How to Enter a Writing Contest and

Win!

✍ ✍ ✍

by
Deepak Gupta

© 2017 by Deepak Gupta. All rights reserved.

Words Matter Publishing
P.O. Box 531
Salem, Il 62881
www.wordsmatterpublishing.com

No part of this publication may be reproduced, stored in a retrieval system, or transmitted in any way by any means—electronic, mechanical, photocopy, recording, or otherwise—without the prior permission of the copyright holder, except as provided by USA copyright law.

ISBN 13: 978-1-947072-22-0
ISBN 10: 1-947072-22-6

Library of Congress Catalog Card Number: 2017955764

Dedication

I want to dedicate this book to my parents, my wife, my son, and Tammy Koelling.

My parents, my wife, and my son are my life.

Tammy Koelling is my inspiration. She inspired me to write this book.

Table of Contents

Introduction to this Guide..1

What Will You Learn in this Guide?......................................2

What is a Writing Contest?...3

Why Should You Enter a Writing Contest?......................5

Benefits of Entering a Writing Contest..............................6

How to Lose a Writing Contest...9

How to Win a Writing Contest...15

What to Do After You Submit Your Manuscript.......37

List of Writing Competitions for 2018...........................39

About the Author...49

Introduction to this Guide

Are you an aspiring author who has been writing a short story, a novel, or a children's book? Maybe you've written a recipe guide, business guide, or a fitness book?

Regardless of the genre, aspiring authors are the future writers of this world. Why shouldn't you become one of them? If you are thinking about writing, you shouldn't wait to start writing tomorrow. By writing every day, you are taking the consistent action necessary to bring your work to fruition and may become a published author much sooner than you think.

Perhaps you feel becoming a successful author is

too difficult? If so, consider the following facts:

- You are knowledgeable about your favorite subject.
- You can turn your daily experiences into words published as a book to help others obtain benefits from your experiences.
- You are able to muster the courage to tell everyone in this world that you are an up and coming author.

So let's make it easy.

You can make your journey to becoming an author more comfortable by participating in some writing contests. DARE to subject your work to careful scrutiny and expert review by entering contests. If your work is accepted, you will take the first giant step towards a successful career as an author!

What will you learn in this guide?

- What is a writing contest?
- Who can enter a writing contest?
- Why you should join a writing contest?
- How to lose a writing contest!
- How to win a writing contest!

What is a Writing Contest?

A writing contest is a competition organized by book publishers, magazine publishers, newspapers, schools, colleges, and so on. Based on who is holding the contest, the theme, the niche, the topics, and the content formatting requirements may vary, so your submission to the writing contest should be made accordingly.

For example, if a book publisher is holding the competition, then it is clear that it is for aspiring authors who want to write and publish their books but are in need of a platform to start.

Thousands of writers can write but;

- They do not know who to contact for a legitimate review of their work.

- They are not aware of the publishers who can help them become an author.
- They think that publishing a book demands thousands of dollars.
- They do not know that by entering their book in a writing contest, not only will it be reviewed, but if they win, their book will be published as well.

So, if you are an aspiring author with an urge to write your book, but you've found it difficult, why not heed the advice of Mary Poppins?

"For every job that must be done, there is an element of fun. You find the fun and 'SNAP,' the job's a game!" Why not "find the fun" and make the job a game by entering a writing contest with the hopes of winning!

Why Should You Enter a Writing Contest?

The reason to enter a writing contest will vary from person to person, but at the end, everyone has one goal, which is to WIN!

If you WIN, you will get prizes, which may include cash rewards, your work being published, and much more. And, if you do not win, so what? You've lost nothing! Instead, you have gained valuable experience which will enable you to do better the next time.

However, "winning" is not the only reason why you should enter the writing contest as there are several benefits.

Benefits of entering a writing contest

- If you have written a novel, a short story, or a yoga guide, then you must want someone to review your work. If you hire a professional proofreader and editor, it may cost you hundreds of dollars, but by submitting your work to a contest, you get it done for free or at a small entry cost. The entry cost comes back to you in many ways, not the least of which being that your work is reviewed for almost nothing.

- There is no need to be afraid as you do not know who is reviewing your book; a professional person will review the work for sure, but as you are not aware of who that person is, there is no need to worry. If he/she finds a lot of mistakes, just relax as everything is behind the curtain!

- You can get feedback on your book without requesting anyone in your circle of friends to read your book and share the feedback.

- You will lose nothing but earn a lot in terms of experience.

- If you are the winner, your book will be

published, and you will become an author!

- If you WIN, you will get the handsome reward.

- Your work will always be yours, as the people who hold the contest cannot use your work in their name. Even if you are not a winner, you can submit your book/article the next time in any other competition.

- You will receive professional feedback showing you how you can improve your writing, formatting of text, etc. And, this can make you a winner of the next contest. So you win, or you learn! Correct?

How to Lose a Writing Contest

If you search for the ways to win a contest, you may find many ideas and concepts shared by several people among whom are professionals and those who have learned much from their journey to success.

While you have many people showing you a way to win a writing contest, have you ever found a person who tells you "how you can lose the contest?"

If not, never fear, I am here!

Being a **Technical Content Writer** and **Editor** since 2007 and a **Book Layout Designer** and **Formatter** since 2011, I have learned a lot during this period. So, you can consider me a learner as well as a professional with many years of experience.

During this period, I even had to cancel some orders and return the money to my clients because they were not happy with my work.

Why did I have to return the money?

It is because I could not understand what their requirements were and how to fulfill them. Sometimes, I offered much better service than what my clients wanted me to do, but going a step above their requirements didn't always suffice. On the other hand, I have made many customers extremely pleased by the extra work that I offered without any additional cost.

So, there are people who may like your additional offerings but also those who want you to do only what you are asked to do. In a contest, however, if you do less or more, you lose. Participating in a contest means you need to do EXACTLY what you are asked to do. If you follow the guidelines; you can win the contest. IF you don't, you won't; it's that simple.

Take a look at these pointers to understand what can cause you to lose the contest.

Contest Guidelines are not completely followed

When someone organizes a contest, he/she wants

it to be a big success; therefore, a list of instructions is prepared. When you submit your work, before even looking at the quality, the very first thing that the reviewer confirms is "that you have followed all the guidelines."

A contest may get 500 or more entries, and many are rejected in the first step because the ***organizers*** do not want to waste their time reviewing the work of the participants who don't even take the ***time*** to read and follow the guidelines.

Grammar rules are ignored

When you are writing a book, it is imperative that you follow grammar rules as per the contest guidelines. If you ignore the rules, you cannot win.

Proofreading is ignored

Even if you are a native English speaker or writer, you cannot ignore proofreading. If you don't proof your work, you have taken a step towards losing the contest.

Why?

It is because even experts can make mistakes like typos. Even if your work is good, if the reviewer has found a few typos, your work may be rejected. Typos are not accepted because it shows that you have not diligently proofread your manuscript.

Not meeting the minimum word count requirement

If you are asked to submit a minimum 5,000 words, but you could barely write 3,000 words, then you are losing the contest. Similarly, if you submit 7,000 words and there is a requirement of a maximum of 6,000 words, you have also lost the contest.

Ignoring the theme and genre

Every writing contest surrounds a theme or genre, and you will be required to submit a manuscript which satisfies this requirement. You may choose to ignore this obligation at your own peril, but you had better be content with losing the contest if you do so. Of course, if losing was your intent, you and the other contestants you have helped by disqualifying yourself, will be jumping with joy.

However, assuming you don't have "time to kill" and a desire to lose, do not ignore these tips. By considering the above-listed pointers, you still won't necessarily win, as winning a writing contest is not that easy. However, at least you have not lost the race by stumbling in the very first steps. If you follow all the guidelines, at the very minimum, your work will be reviewed by the organizers, and your writing journey has begun successfully, perhaps even culminating in you winning the competition!

How to Win a Writing Contest

Nobody can share the tips and strategies that will guarantee your victory because no such thing exists in this world. The tips, guidance, and strategies are only leading you in the right direction. What you do after taking those initial steps will have a much more decided impact on your success or defeat.

So, I am here to share some tips that you can follow to strengthen your chances of winning the contest.

In this book, I am specifically sharing tips about the writing contests that are organized by publishers, which means apart from your writing, the formatting of your manuscript will be critical.

Let's have a look at the tips.

1 – Read the contest guidelines

I have already stated this point, but I am iterating it again here because it is the first and most important point to pave a clear path to your triumph. So, in no case, can you avoid a single guideline, even if you have already participated in many contests, and are aware of some common guidelines.

Read every instruction twice before you start writing the content, and before you submit your work, make certain that you have met all the guidelines.

2 – Read the theme/genre

The contest is always ran around a theme or a genre. So, carefully read the theme/genre and then decide if you are comfortable with writing a short story around that theme/genre.

I suggest that if you are not confident at this step, then STOP now otherwise you will end up wasting your precious time. For example, if you are a fitness trainer and can write a good book on fitness, but the theme is related to gardening or romance, then do not accept the challenge. Rather, look for the other contests offering you a chance in the theme/genre you are comfortable pursuing.

3 – Read submission guidelines

Every contest has many guidelines–from how to write, what to write, etc., to other various regulations regarding submission. It is your duty to ensure that you meet all the guidelines if you want to win.

So, before you submit your story for review, read the submission guidelines and meet them accordingly.

4 – Start writing in the requested application

After you have read all guidelines, you can start writing the story.

WAIT!

Have you read what application they want you to use for your entry? Do they want you to submit a Word doc? OR, are you also allowed to use Google Docs or any other such online Word editor? Can you also use Open Office?

Are you allowed to submit a PDF?

Or, are you bound to send a Word doc only?

I have included this step here because while reading the guidelines; you may have noticed the document format they want you to submit. Based on that format, you need to decide the application you can select to write the story.

If they want you to **submit a PDF**, that's good news because you can use any word editor that allows you to create a PDF. However, if they have specifically requested you to submit your work in **.doc** or **.docx** formats, then you are bound to use Microsoft Word only.

If you ignore this point and submit a PDF, then you have disqualified yourself from the contest even before it has started.

5 – Write an engaging title

Once you have decided on the application, let's start writing the story. You must have a catchy title that you want for your book.

This is a critical first step and could decide how engaging your story will be.

Also, if you want people to read your story, then you need to give them a reason to hold the book, read its title, open it up and start reading the book.

You can make that happen by writing a captivating title. Also, if your title is appealing, the reviewer will be impressed at first glance, and when this happens, the reviewer is in an excellent mood, which is an added bonus for you.

So, think hard about the title. Keep thinking some more until you decide on the best possible one to suit your book.

6 – Write your story – keep it within the suggested word limit

The word limit is set to make the contest more challenging. For some people, writing a great story within the requested word count is easy, while for others, the word limit handicaps them from developing their story the way they would like.

However, a contest simply cannot allow you to submit a story without a minimum and maximum word count. You cannot send a story in just 500 words. By the same token, you cannot submit a story in 500,000 words.

You first need to check the word limit for the contest. If the set word limit is 2,000-2,500 words, then your story should be completed within that range; no less and no more.

7 – Make your story impressive with your writing

You have written an engaging title, but that's not enough. You need to put life in your story also. You have impressed the reviewer with a great title, but now you need to ensure that your story touches the heart of the reviewer. If this happens, your chances of winning the contest will increase exponentially.

How can you do this?

First of all, ensure that your story is on track with the title. If there is no sync between the title and the content, you are in trouble.

You need to ensure that you are not missing the flow when moving from one paragraph to the next and from one chapter to the next.

Create a Table of Contents to give the reader an idea of what is in the book.

8 – Proofread once you are done with the writing

Once the writing has been completed, it is the time to proofread and edit your work. Read again and again to make sure of the following:

- There are no grammatical errors
- There are no typos
- There are no double spaces
- There are no loose sentences
- Sentence formation is good
- Chapter ends perfectly
- The story concludes with a finish
- If you want to create a sequel to the book, make sure there are elements in the story which can be expanded upon later, but also make sure that the conclusion of your first book does not appear too dangling.

To find and fix typos and common grammar errors, you can use any professional service. For example, if you are writing in MS Word, use its spell and grammar check feature to fix typos and grammar issues.

If you have the budget, you can use a **grammar checker** tool like **Grammarly** – it is known as one of the best tools to help you fix grammar mistakes and typos.

9 – Ready to submit? Wait and check the style, font, etc.

When everything is ready, and you are confident that you have done a superb job with words, let me tell you that if the formatting of your document is not correct, you are losing the battle.

You may receive good feedback about the story, but you cannot be a winner because the formatting was incorrect, or you may not have even formatted the document.

What exactly is this "formatting" all about?

One of the most important points that you must make absolutely sure you don't miss is checking that you have formatted the manuscript correctly.

Formatting is a process to organize your book in proper sections, making it easy to read.

A writing contest does not mean you can submit your story in a raw format, which looks like a big heap of words.

You need to make sure that it is easy for the reviewer to navigate through the story. The document you are going to submit must be correctly formatted and arranged to leave a first good impression on the reviewer before he/she actually starts reviewing your work.

If you read any novel or book, you will see that it has a title page, a table of contents, headers, footers, chapter headings, chapter content, and the end as well.

You may have noticed that a chapter always starts on a new page, and never ends with just a single to a few words on a page.

You may have also noticed that the chapter title is bigger than the rest of the chapter content.

This arrangement of the content is called the formatting.

In some contests, you are also provided with the guidelines to format your document before submission. These guidelines may include but not be limited to the following:

- Font type and size for the book title
- Font type and size for the author name on the title page
- Font type and size for the chapter title
- Font type and size for the chapter text
- Font type and size for the header and footer

- Paragraph line spacing
- Space between two paragraphs
- Additional styling like adding drop cap, images, etc.
- Where to add the author name in the header – (on the left side of the page or right side)
- Where to add the book title in the header – (on the left side of the page or right side)

If you see any such guidelines, then make sure that you implement them before submitting the document.

If you do not see any guidelines, then you should always use a common font like Times New Roman or Calibri for your document.

The book title page can be about 18 pt. and bold while the author name can be 14 pt. and bold.

You can keep the size of the chapter title as 14 pt. bold, and line spacing can be 1.2-1.5. Do not use double spacing as double spacing is not easy for the eyes of the reader due to too much space between the lines.

The font size for the chapter text can be 12 pt., and the space after paragraph can be 10 pt.

The book title should be on the right-hand side of the header while the author's name should be on the left-hand side.

These are some general formatting guidelines that you will want to follow to increase your chances of winning the contest. However, as I already stated, nobody, including myself, can guarantee your victory, but you are doing yourself and the reviewer a big favor by following and meeting the contest guidelines.

10 – Have you added styles to your manuscript (story)?

You can make your manuscript (story) look attractive by adding styles to it.

What does a style mean?

It means you can use some eye-catching fonts, different designs for heading 1, heading 2, and so on, and you can make use of ornaments such as flowers, heart's, etc. as well.

Some examples of ornaments are;

Moreover, you can add text boxes with designer borders. Page borders can be added as well, and many other things can be done to make your document look more visually pleasing.

BUT

Before you add any style to your story, go back to the contest guidelines, read them once again, and confirm that you are allowed to add a style.

Adding styles to your manuscript depends upon the contest requirement.

If you are not allowed to add any style but must use only simple formatting, then respect the guidelines. However, if you are asked to add styles to your manuscript, which may happen in the case that the theme is related to romance or poetry, go ahead and make your manuscript look more appealing.

Some Formatting Examples are given below:

Example of the Book Title page with an Ornament

You can see that the Word "WIN!" has been written in bigger font than other words.

Also, an ornament has been used to make the page look interesting. You can also do something like this, if allowed.

How to Enter a Writing Contest
and
Win!

✍ ✍ ✍

by
Deepak Gupta

Example of Chapter title with Underline and Ornament.

You can see that the Chapter title has been made bigger, and given a center alignment. Plus, an underline has been added. And, to make it look like the start of a new section, a beautiful ornament has been added.

You can also do this but only when the contest allows you.

🏆 🏆 🏆

Example of the first paragraph of every chapter

You can even make the start of every chapter pretty interesting and attractive by adding some additional styles to you first paragraph. For example, if you look at the below image, you will notice that I have added a dropcap style to the first letter of the first paragraph of the chapter.

Adding the dropcap style has made the start of the chapter fascinating. Right?

> Nobody can share the tips and strategies that will guarantee your victory because no such thing exists in this world. The tips, guidance, and strategies are only leading you in the right direction. What you do after taking those initial steps will have a much more decided impact on your success or defeat.
>
> So, I am here to share some tips that you can follow to strengthen your chances of winning the contest.
>
> In this book, I am specifically sharing tips about the writing contests that are organized by publishers,

So, these are some examples related to book formatting, which you may want to implement in your manuscript while organizing it. However, again I want to insist that you first read the guidelines, and add a style only when you are allowed to do that.

11 – Proofread once again

So, everything has now been completed. You have written the story, proofread it, formatted it, and looked at the submission guidelines as well.

Has something been missed?

Yes, everything has been completed, but still, one more round of proofreading is required.

It is human nature that whenever you read your story, you may find some typos, if not typos, then possibly double spaces or grammar issues. Nobody in this world is perfect so you should again proofread your manuscript before you give it a final approval and submit it.

12 – Have you carefully filled out the submission form?

You cannot just email your work to the contest organizers asking them to review it and to send the feedback to you at the same email address.

Organizers always look for dedicated writers, so they always request some information from them. They often provide them a form to fill out and sign. Once the submission form has been filled out, you can send your manuscript along with that form.

Every field in the submission form is important so you should not miss or ignore any of them. Some organizers may even ask you to provide them with your physical address, mobile phone number, and more details so that they can make sure that you are a serious candidate for them.

Those who do not show interest in filling out the submission form correctly, stand a greater chance of losing the contest. Why? Simply because the submission form is the very first thing that the organizers look at before even deciding to look at your story. Why risk hurting your chances by being careless at what should be the easiest part of the process?

Follow the guidelines listed above, and you will

greatly increase your chances of winning the writing contest.

What to Do After You Submit Your Manuscript

After you have submitted your manuscript for a review, it is time you to relax.

Take a break!

Chill with friends!

Then go back to work. Start preparing for the next contest with an excellent idea and theme and make winning every competition a habit.

You should not just sit around waiting for the results of the contest because the results will be declared as stated in the guidelines. Why waste your precious time? Use it to win another contest!

If you have thought about writing the sequel to your previously submitted manuscript, begin working on that.

If you win, your first release will be published, and if you lose, do not be disheartened. Rather, realize you have taken the important initial step in becoming a published author. Accept the help offered by the organizers of the contest and get your work published by them after implementing their feedback in the manuscript.

Sometimes, it may be that your work is good, but the winner's work was just a bit better in the eyes of the contest organizers. In this case, you have received valuable feedback from them. So even if you've lost the contest, you have won! You have been receptive to their expert advice, made appropriate changes and now you can straightforwardly request them to publish your work and help you become an author who has his/her book available for sale at Amazon.com and many other websites and stores.

List of Writing Competitions for 2018

✍ ✍ ✍

After reading the book, you might be expecting a list of "Writing Competitions" that you can join. So, here is the list of some of the "Writing Competitions for 2018."

Note:

Please note that the information provided about the competitions is taken from the respective websites, so may change without any notice. It is suggested to visit the given links to check the latest information about the contest and guidelines.

The source of the information of these contest is Google and the respective websites of the companies/institutes running these competitions.

#1 - Words Matter Publishing's Book Writing Contests, Poetry Contests and Short Story Contests

Words Matter Publishing was founded by T.S. Koelling, a ghostwriter. Being a ghostwriter herself, she understands the importance of words that you put together to shape your book. So, to award the hard work of writers, she runs book writing competitions.

Her upcoming competitions will be **a Book Writing Contest, Poetry Contest, and Short Story Contest** that you can enter by simply purchasing books or other items from the WMP Book Boutique. **Winners of the Book Writing Contest** will receive a book publishing contract with them that includes an effective layout designing of your book in both Print and Ebook, Book Trailer, and Marketing as well. For a total value of **$12,000. Winners of the Poetry Contest** will receive a 1st, 2nd, or 3rd place ribbon to place on your submission. When enough submissions have been received a book will be published with winning the entries. **Winners of the Short Story Contest** will also receive a 1st, 2nd, or 3rd place ribbon and will be published in a book when enough entries have been received to make a compilation.

Visit https://wordsmatterpublishing.com/ to

check the competition details and how to enroll.

#2 - The Fiction Desk Ghost Story Competition

The entries for 2018 Ghost Story Competition are open here. Deadline to enter the contest is January 31, 2018. You will need to pay £8 per story as the entry cost. And, the prizes are as below:

- First prize of £500
- Second prize of £250
- Third prize of £100

Visit http://www.thefictiondesk.com/submissions/ghost-story-competition.php for more details

#3 - Hub City Press $10,000 C. Michael Curtis Short Story Book Contest

It is a book writing contest, and the winner will get an excellent prize. The entries are open, and the deadline is January 1, 2018. The entry fee is $25. The first winning book of this contest will be published in Spring 2019.

Your submission will be judged by **Lee K. Abbott,** author of seven collections of short stories.

Visit https://hubcity.org/news/2017/hub-city-announces-10-000-c-michael-curtis-prize for more details

#4 - Women's National Book Association Writing Contest

Submissions for this contest are open. The deadline to apply for this contest is March 1, 2018. The prize is $250, and the entry fee is $15 for the members of WNBA, and if you not a member of WNBA, then the entry fee is $20.

Available categories are Fiction, non-fiction, Poetry, and Young Adult fiction.

Visit http://www.wnba-books.org/contest/ for more details

#5 - Flyway Notes From The Field Contest

The submissions are open. There are many contests for different categories, and the deadline is January 1, 2018, to May 1, 2018. The entry fee is $12. And, the winning prize is $500 plus publication in a future issue of Flyway. The best part of this competition is that all submissions may be considered for publication.

Visit https://flyway.submittable.com/submit for more details

#6 - St. Martin's Minotaur/ Mystery Writers of America First Crime Novel Competition

Submissions for this contest are open. The deadline to apply for this contest is January 12, 2018. There is no entry fee to enter this contest. This is a big competition where you need to submit about 60, 000 words in the English language. The theme is Crime. The winner will receive an advance against future royalties of $10,000

Visit http://mysterywriters.org/about-mwa/st-martins/ for more details

#7 - Everything Change Climate Fiction Contest 2018

Submissions for this contest are open. The deadline to apply for this contest is February 28, 2018. It is a fiction writing contest where you need to submit your work in 5000 words. The submission fee is $0, which means Entry is free. The winner will get $1000 as prize money, and the nine finalists will also get $50 in prize money.

Visit https://everythingchange.submittable.com/submit for more details

#8 - Palooka Press Contest

Submissions for this contest are open. The deadline to apply for this contest is May 15, 2018. The entry fee is $10. All types of manuscripts between 30-50 pages are welcome. The prize is the publication of your book with $300 honorarium plus 20 free copies of the book.

Visit http://palookamag.com/palooka-press for more details

#9 – Reedsy Prompts Short Story Contest

Submissions for this contest are open. The deadline to apply for this contest is December 31st, 2018. The entry fee is $0, which means free. You stand a chance to win $50.

Visit https://reedsy.com/writing for more details

#10 – The Killer Nashville Claymore Award

Submissions for this contest are open. The deadline to apply for this contest is April 1, 2018. The entry fee is $40. You will get a chance to win the publishing contract. They have a big list of prizes. Every year they distribute rewards worth $3000. Multiple genres are allowed like Action, Adventure, Alternate History, Fantasy, Horror, Mystery, Sci-Fi, Speculative, Suspense, Thriller, and Western manuscripts.

Visit https://blog.reedsy.com/writing-contests/ for more details

#11 – Stella Kupferberg Memorial Short Story Prize

Submissions for this contest are open. The deadline to apply for this contest is March 1, 2018. The entry fee is $25. Jess Walter, author of Beautiful Ruins, will judge your work. The winner will get $1000 and a free 10-week course with Gotham Writers.

Visit https://www.writingclasses.com/contest/stella-kupferberg-memorial-short-story-prize-2018 for more details

#12 – Very Short Fiction Award

Submissions for this contest are open. The deadline to apply for this contest is January 2, 2018. The entry fee is $16. The winner will get $2000. The second winner will get $500, and if the work is accepted for publication, then $700 along with 10 copies. The third winner will get $300, and if the work is accepted for publication, then $700 along with 10 copies.

Visit https://glimmertrainpressinc.submittable.com/submit/92255/nov-dec-2017-very-short-fiction-award for more details

#13 – Marsh Hawk Press Poetry

It is a poetry competition for which submissions are open. The deadline to apply for this contest is April 30, 2018. The entry fee is $25. The winner will get $1000 as cash prize plus publication of work. The manuscript should be about 48 to 84 pages.

Visit https://marshhawkpressinc.submittable.com/submit for more details

#14 – Bath Flash Fiction Award Novella-in-Flash Award

The submissions are open for this competition. The deadline to apply for this contest is January 29, 2018. The entry fee is $16. The winner will get £300 prize, and two runner-ups will get the prizes of £100.

Visit https://bathflashfictionaward.com/ for more details

#15 – Cleveland State University's First Book Poetry Competition

The submissions are open for this competition. The deadline to apply for this contest is March 31, 2018. The entry fee is $28. The manuscript should be a minimum 48 pages.

Visit http://www.csupoetrycenter.com/first-book-poetry/ for more details

#16 – Inkitt Novel Competition

The submissions are open for this competition. The deadline to apply for this contest is January 30, 2018. The entry fee is $0. The genre is fiction. The winner will get the publication contract along with 51% royalties on print books and 25% royalties on eBook.

Visit https://www.inkitt.com/novelcontest for more details

#17 – The David Nathan Meyerson Prize for Fiction

The submissions are open for this competition. The deadline to apply for this contest is May 1, 2018. The entry fee is $25. The winner will get the publication contract in SWR and $1000 prize.

Visit http://www.smu.edu/SouthwestReview/Prizes-and-Awards/MeyersonFictionPrize for more details

#18 – Nimrod Literary Awards

The submissions will start on January 1, 2018. The deadline to apply for this contest is April 30, 2018. The entry fee is $20. The winner will get the publication contract and $2000 prize. The second winner will get $1000 plus a publishing contract.

Visit https://nimrod.utulsa.edu/awards.html for more details

#19 – Snowbound Chapbook Award of Tupelo Press

The submissions are open. The deadline to apply for this contest is February 28, 2018. The entry fee is $25. The winner will get the publication contract for 25 copies and $1000 prize.

Visit https://www.tupelopress.org/snowbound-chapbook-award/ for more details

#20 – Walt Whitman Award

The submissions are open. The deadline to apply for this contest is November 1, 2018. The entry fee is $35. The winner will get $5000 prize publication by Graywolf Press.

Visit https://www.poets.org/academy-american-poets/prizes/walt-whitman-award for more details

About the Author

Deepak Gupta is a writer by profession in the technical domain. Apart from technical content writing, he has expertise into book layout designing, pagination, and formatting. He can help you turn your simple manuscript into a professional book in both print and ebook (epub, kindle, and print PDF) formats.

He is a big time foodie and loves to explore authentic recipes (only pure veg.). In his free time, he likes watching comedy TV shows, movies, and listening to music.

For feedback on the formatting and designing of this book, you can reach him at

guptadeepak2353@gmail.com

or

contact@vanzzsolutions.com

Also, you can use the same approach to contact him if you need him to design, paginate, and format your book.

The End

Coming Books

An Ultimate Guide to Increase Sales via Twitter

www.ingramcontent.com/pod-product-compliance
Lightning Source LLC
Chambersburg PA
CBHW071544080526
44588CB00011B/1792